Pre-Engagement

5 Questions to Ask Yourselves

Resources for Changing Lives

A Ministry of
THE CHRISTIAN COUNSELING AND
EDUCATIONAL FOUNDATION
Glenside, Pennsylvania

RCL Ministry Booklets
Susan Lutz, Series Editor

Pre-Engagement

5 Questions to Ask Yourselves

David Powlison
and
John Yenchko

P&R PUBLISHING
P.O. BOX 817 • PHILLIPSBURG • NEW JERSEY 08865-0817

Printed in the United States of America

ISBN 10: 0-87552-679-9
ISBN 13: 978-0-87552-679-9

Do you remember the Fram oil filter commercial on TV a few years back? The mechanic stands between two cars. One car is in for an oil change and routine maintenance; the other is a smoking wreck with a blown engine. "There's the easy way and the hard way to keep your car working," says the mechanic. "You can pay me now . . . or you can pay me later." The cost to you now is only the cost of a filter. The cost later is a whole lot more: a complete engine overhaul because of your lack of preventive maintenance.

When you are thinking about getting married, you ought to approach it with the same wisdom and foresight as the man who was wise enough to replace his oil filter!

That doesn't mean there is no place for romance and a special "click" between two people. But in actually choosing to get married there are a number of basic questions that you should ask first. There is "preventive maintenance" that can keep you from coming in with a "blown engine" later. After all, only if the engine is running smoothly can you enjoy the wind in your hair!

We will give you and your potential fiancé(e) five questions you can ask yourselves and discuss together. Answering these will help you decide on solid grounds, "Should we get married?" We are convinced that the time to ask yourselves some serious questions is *before* you ask that most serious question, "Will you marry me?" Answering these questions now, before you make the commitment, can prevent the pain of major repair work later.

1. Are You Both Christians?

Marriage is a "covenant of companionship." Two people pull together in the same harness. If two people have God first in their lives, they are able to answer with confidence, "Yes, we both know Jesus as our Savior and follow him as our Lord."

Under Christ's lordship you will be able to face with confidence whatever comes your way. Have you believed in Jesus, the unique Son of God the Father, who died in your place, who was raised from the dead to give you the Holy Spirit and the power of a new life, and who will return to give you an immortal life with him?

Being a Christian means that these truths shine in your heart so that you know God and receive his love. Being a Christian is more than a verbal profession of faith in Jesus Christ. It is a way of life. It means in practice that you love and rely on Jesus more than on your spouse. Are you *living* as a Christian? Or are you making marriage more important than Jesus? Ask—for yourself and for your prospective spouse—"Is Jesus really my Lord?" Is he your number-one priority? The master you listen to? The one you trust more than anything or anyone else?

There are at least four ways in which Jesus' lordship can be compromised when it comes to deciding whether or not to get married.

First, are you looking to marriage to make you happy or complete, to give you identity or purpose? When this happens, Christ is no longer your Lord in a practical way.

Marriage is a wonderful gift from God, but it cannot take God's place. Do you think getting married will provide meaning in your life? Direction? Security? Self-respect? Do you hope marriage will remove a sense of despair, inadequacy, failure, bitterness, or isolation? Do you say to yourself, "If only I could find a husband, then I'd be happy," or "I can finally find love, acceptance, and security if I get married," or "My life is a failure unless I get married"? If so, you are asking too much of marriage.

People often come to marriage with such unrealistic expectations. Marriage will shape and affect your life in many ways, but do not expect marriage to do what only Jesus can do. Unrealistic and distorted views of marriage will lead to disappointment, frustration, anger, and despair when your partner lets you down and proves to have "feet of clay."

Do you think that marriage will be your source of joy and happiness? Is it going to make your life "come together"? There is no question that marriage *is* a blessing. It is the richest and closest human relationship we can enjoy. In a good marriage there is the potential to receive many good things: intimate friendship, encouragement, sexual joy, the satisfaction of working in partnership, children, and the freedom to be yourself that comes when you are fully known *and* fully accepted by someone.

But your spouse will not solve your personal problems or fulfill all your desires. Marriage must first be a place where you are committed to learn how to *give* blessing, even when the going is tough. If you build your life on the promises and gifts of God in Jesus Christ, you will be able not only to weather storms but to grow through the storms into greater maturity and love.

Be honest with yourself. Deep down, are you looking to marriage for what you hope to get from it?

Or are you aware of what you must give, because you have already gotten from God what you really need? "In everything, do to others what you would have them do to you" (Matt. 7:12). Of course, you want the blessings of a good marriage, but do you want even more to build your own life on Jesus, and then give those blessings to your spouse? This way of life is the only "house built on a rock," able to keep standing when disappointments come. The traditional vows express this well: "For better or for worse, for richer or for poorer, in sickness and in health, to love and to cherish, till death us do part."

Second, are you thinking of marrying a non-Christian?

The Bible clearly teaches that Christians should not be "unequally yoked" (2 Cor. 6:14–16 KJV).

We have met people who waffle at this point. They try to excuse going against Jesus' lordship, which raises real questions about their own commitment to Christ. The black-and-white view of 2 Corinthians 6:14–16—righteousness and wickedness, light and dark, Christ and the devil, belief and unbelief, God and idolatry—is rather hard to miss!

If you choose to marry against Christ, then romance, infatuation, your desires for marriage, or your fears of not being married have taken control of your life. That is idolatry. The professing Christian is actually being tempted to choose the "dark" side of 2 Corinthians 6. You think that what is actually worst for you will be best.

A more subtle version of this problem occurs when you want to marry someone whose profession of faith is suspect. We have often encountered the situation where a man who does not love Christ wants to marry a woman who is a Christian. In the course of their relationship, he finds that she will only marry another Christian, so he thinks, "Fine, I can go along with you and join your church."

What is happening here? His ulterior motive is to win the girl, not to give his life to the Lord. Once again, the couple will be unequally yoked. You must establish as a reality that Jesus Christ is more important than either marriage or the other person. Far from hindering your joy in life, this will lead you to greater joy and spare you much pain.

Third, does either of you have complicating entanglements from past marriages or relationships?

We live in a society of "easy come, easy go." Marriage, sex, and children are not viewed with the sanctity with which the Lord Jesus views them. If Christ is the Lord of your life, you need to determine, according to his Word, whether he says you are free to marry or remarry now.

There are "legal" divorces that Jesus views as illegitimate (Matt. 19:1–9). There are times when the Lord commands us to continue to pursue reconciliation rather than remarry (1 Cor. 7:10–11). There are also situations where the marriage is viewed by God as broken, and a person is free to consider remarrying (Matt. 5:31–32; Rom. 7:2–3; 1 Cor. 7:12–16, 39). All the ins and outs of these questions go beyond the scope of our discussion here. But if you have prior entanglements (a prior marriage, children out of wedlock, etc.) you must think through the implications of what the Lord says. Seek pastoral counsel from others who will take the biblical passages seriously. Ideally, the church should make a declaration that a person is or is not free to remarry.

Fourth, has God given you the gift of singleness?

God sometimes calls people to a fruitful life of ministry as a single person. This possibility is discussed by two very well known singles, Jesus and Paul! (See Matt. 19:11–12; 1 Cor. 7:1–9, 17–40.)

Unmarried persons can devote themselves to the affairs of the kingdom of God without the responsibilities to a husband or wife and children. Marriage has a cost: "Those who marry will face many troubles in this life," as Paul writes in 1 Corinthians 7:28.

A single person, using his or her singleness well, has a flexibility and freedom to do things a married person cannot consider. Remember, for over a thousand years the "ideal" Christian was unmarried! Celibacy was perhaps overvalued in the medieval church, to the detriment of marriage. But in our society the church usually goes to the opposite extreme. Some of the most fruitful ministries in the contemporary church are based on the freedom that singleness gives.

In our own local church, we see singles uniquely able to meet difficult counseling needs, to get involved with teenagers, to give time to the poor or to refugees, to help others with moving or house painting or child care. An unmarried person can have the time to volunteer in a local hospital or nursing home or to get involved in political activity. Unmarried people with good jobs are free of many financial pressures that families feel, and they are freed for generosity. One single person we know has even set up a small foundation to give away a large percentage of his salary.

It may well be that you have the gift of marriage. In this case you will thrive best by seeking to establish a family. But take time to think whether you may have the gift of singleness. What are your ministry gifts and opportunities? How strong is your sexual drive, and how well do you have it under control? How important are children to you and to what you do best? What are the advantages, as well as disadvantages, of remaining unmarried? What would be some of the "costs," as well as benefits, of getting married?

Marriage is a great gift. But it is not the greatest gift, nor does it provide the deepest and surest joys. The greatest gift is Jesus. So make sure that he is first in both of your lives. With him as the foundation, you will enjoy building a relationship of enduring love with your brother or sister in the Lord.

For Discussion

1. Jesus Christ is called "Savior" and "Lord." What do these mean in your life?
2. How do you pray about marriage? Is it "Lord, give me a spouse and then I'll be happy"? Or is it "Lord, help me to be a better person, more worth marrying"?
3. Are you pretending to be a Christian in order to get a husband or wife?
4. Have you made a public profession of faith in a Bible-believing church?
5. Are you both free of prior entanglements from past marriages or relationships?
6. Does either of you have the gift of singleness? Would marriage help or hinder your usefulness to the Lord?

2. Do You Have a Track Record of Solving Problems Biblically?

Problems come up in every relationship. How do you handle them? Because we are all sinners with problems, none of us has a perfect track record here. If you are honest, you will likely answer "Sometimes" or "No" to this question. But the key is not perfection. Rather, is your "no" becoming "sometimes" and is your "sometimes" becoming "more times"? Is there a growing "yes"? The focus is on your maturity. The question of your maturity for marriage has three parts:

1. Do you *know* how to solve problems biblically?
2. Do you *do* it?
3. If not, where do you need to *change* and grow?

In Matthew 7:24–27 Jesus says, "Everyone who hears these words of mine and puts them into practice is like a wise man who built his house on the rock. The rain came down, the streams rose, and the winds blew and beat against that house; yet it did not fall, because it had its foundation on the rock." Jesus speaks of knowing his words, the Bible. But that, of course, is not enough. He speaks of putting them into practice. Problems will come, but if you learn to face them his way, he promises you will stand.

First, do you know how to solve problems biblically?

A pre-engaged couple can't anticipate every problem, of course. But do you have a general awareness of how the Bible speaks practically to the major areas of life: commitment, communication, forgiving each other, facing adversity, sexual relations, child-rearing, finances, etc.? The Bible *does* speak to these things! You ought to know something about what it says and be willing to learn more.

A Christian couple who had been married for fifteen years came in for counseling because of severe marital problems. After several sessions, the wife sheepishly confessed that she had never known that the Bible said she should make her husband a priority! Many years of pain, loneliness, and misunderstanding could have been prevented if they had started their marriage the Lord's way.

Second, do you do what the Bible says?

This takes you out of the realm of theory and makes you look at what you really do! What is your usual pattern of addressing problems? Failure to solve problems biblically shows up in lots of obvious ways. Are you a bully? Do you manipulate? Do you avoid facing problems? Do you let things slide until you forget about them? Do you whitewash matters by pretending everything is okay? Do you store up resentments? Are you a sulker? Do you blame-shift and make excuses, always pointing the finger at the other person or at circumstances? Do you keep on doing things the Bible says are wrong?

Or have you learned the basic skills of how to solve problems? Do you bring things up and talk them through? Do you go to Christ for help? Do you take time to think about what the right thing is to do? Do you ask forgiveness for your side of the problem no matter what the other person did? Do you strive to forgive? Do you pray together? After you have forgiven, do you let the past go and express love to each other again? Do you keep the lines of communication open to prevent problems from developing? To enjoy the blessings in marriage, you need skills in solving problems and building honesty and trust.

Third, where do you need to change and grow to become a wiser person?

If you do not have a track record of solving problems biblically, it does not mean you should immediately end the friendship. But it does mean that the caution flag is out and you must work—together and in pre-engagement counseling—on your problem areas.

We are very serious about this. Are there patterns of sin in your lives? Are you tempting each other sexually? Are you critical or cruel towards each other verbally or physically? Do you lie? Are you putting on a front and concealing areas of your past or present? Do you spend money impulsively? Are you bitter at your parents? Do you have any extreme fears? In a nutshell, have you dealt with your own sins and the sins of others against you?

You need to be honest with yourself and your potential mate, facing these things in the light of the mercy and grace of Jesus Christ. These are areas in which we grow. If there is no growth but problems continue unresolved with one or both parties, then you should not marry. We are not speaking of perfection—who could ever get married?!—but of meaningful, moving-in-the-right-direction progress.

Why Are We So Concerned About This?

Problem patterns don't go away when you get married. Instead, they are aggravated, and the painful consequences multiply. For example, a single man with a temper problem may be annoying and obnoxious at times to his friends. But he will be frightening and dangerous to his wife and children. If the temper is dealt with before engagement, pain and heartache will be avoided. A man who has learned that his will is not God, who has learned to be honest and own up to his sins, and who is growing in self-control will make a husband worth marrying.

We've painted the dark side so far. There is also a beautiful side that accompanies an honest "yes" to the question, "Do you have a track record of solving problems biblically?"

Positive patterns also remain when you get married. If you have faced even small rough spots together and have seen honesty, compassion, kindness, patience, and trust grow between you, then you have reason to expect that God's Spirit will continue to work these fruits of the Spirit into your lives.

We need to highlight two other aspects of growing Christian maturity. First, prayer is the most direct expression of dependency on God. So, what is your prayer life like, both individually and together? No prayer? No dependency. Self-centered prayer? God is your errand boy. True prayer? "Blessed are the poor in spirit, for theirs is the kingdom of heaven" (Matt. 5:3). Have you learned to seek God's face together? Are you asking him to make his kingdom the organizing center of your life? Ask him to bless your relationship, whether or not it ends in marriage. Ask him to give you wisdom and grace to decide whether or not to marry.

Another key issue concerns your sexual morality as unmarried people. Dating couples often sin against each other sexually. The often-asked question "How far can we go before we sin?" is not hard to answer. What expressions of affection would be appropriate for you to express to your own sister or brother? In God's eyes there are only two basic kinds of loving relationships between men and women. Almost all members of the opposite sex are to be considered as your "family" and loved in ways appropriate to family; that is, nonsexually. Only one person, your husband or wife, can be in the other category, "spouse." With this person God delights in calling you to love in ways appropriate to a one-flesh relationship—that is, sexually. He even commands it (Prov. 5:18)!

In other words, all women except one—your wife—are in the category of mother, grandmother, sister, daughter. Your girlfriend or fiancée is a "sister" first of all and should be treated as such. All men except one—your husband—are in the category of father, grandfather, brother, son. Your boyfriend or fiancé is a "brother" until you marry. Anything that sexualizes such familial relationships violates love.

The question "How far can we go?" is actually the wrong question. You should instead be asking, "How can we honor, respect, and encourage each other's purity and not tempt each other to sin?" If you are able to love each other in this area before you are married, your foundation for joyous, trusting marital sexuality will be strong, and you will be prepared for the seasons of abstinence that necessarily arise on occasion in marriage.

No one has a problem-free marriage. But the couple with a record of solving problems biblically can have confidence that Jesus Christ is active in their lives. As they are attentive to his voice in the nitty-gritty hardships of life, they know that by God's grace they have what they need to keep their commitment and solve their problems.

For Discussion

1. List three problems or disagreements you have faced in the past. Discuss how you dealt with them.

2. List three problems you now face, and discuss how you propose to solve them biblically.

3. Study together Galatians 5:13–6:10. In your lives, where do you find sinful tendencies? Where do you find love?

4. Discuss your prayer and devotional life. What is it like individually? What is it like together?

5. Discuss how you are treating each other sexually. Read 1 Timothy 5:1–2, and notice how all nonmarried relationships are characterized in familial terms. Notice the particular exhortation to Timothy, an unmarried man, to treat younger women "as sisters, with all purity" (KJV). Do you need to seek forgiveness from each other and redefine the lines according to love rather than desire?

3. Are You Heading in the Same Direction in Life?

When the Bible speaks of marriage, it speaks four times of "leaving and cleaving." Leaving means you are tied no longer to the direction set by your parents and your single life. Cleaving means you choose to move in the same direction as your spouse.

Certainly there will never be total agreement and uniformity between two people. After all, you are not marrying yourself but someone who will complement you! We are not arguing for the secular notion of "compatibility," that you both have to come hatched out of the same mold. Two very different people can have a wonderful marriage. But there are basic kinds of agreement that a man and woman must come to in order to cleave to one another.

This calls you to make a realistic assessment of your similarities and differences and to make realistic choices and plans about the future. Jesus says that we must count the cost of our decisions (Luke 14:28–29). Any couple contemplating marriage should ask "leaving and cleaving" questions of themselves. Look at each other realistically and objectively.

Leaving Questions

Are you willing to make a break emotionally with your parents?

Failure to do this leads to such problems as: the man who visits his mother every day before returning home to his wife; the man who won't defend his wife against criticism by his parents; the woman who insists that all vacations be taken with her parents; the woman who "goes home to mother"—by phone or physical visit—at the first sign of difficulty. Leaving your parents means you build a new family unit.

Are you willing to make a break financially? Are you taking responsibility to care for yourselves and pay your own way?

Are you willing to break with your friends and your single life? The man can't go out three nights a week with the guys. The woman cannot make her best friends the source of all her emotional and spiritual satisfaction.

Are you willing to break with your job? In our career-oriented world, do you understand that your spouse comes before your job, and you cannot neglect your spouse for the sake of work or study?

Are you willing to break with the right that single people have to make independent decisions, keep their own counsel, go as they please, and maintain the degree of privacy they choose? To choose to "leave" is to choose to become "one flesh" with another person. You open your life. You make joint decisions. First Corinthians 7 teaches that there is a cost—loss of individual freedom—in gaining the intimacy and partnership of marriage.

Obviously each of these hard questions needs to be properly balanced. In each of these questions we do not mean "break" in an absolute sense. Rather you need fundamentally to re-arrange your priorities, values, and commitments with your spouse at the center. Certainly you will love your parents; there are appropriate ways parents might help you out; you will not ignore your friends; you will go to work; you will remain an individual. But in each case there is a redefinition of the place these things have in your life.

Cleaving Questions

Where are you going in your life? What are your gifts and ministry interests? What are you doing with your life to serve the Lord? Can you walk alongside each other gladly? What kind of job do you have or anticipate?

What is your basic lifestyle? What are your work hours and habits? How do you like to spend leisure and recreational time? How do you spend Saturdays? When do you go to bed and wake up? How much TV do you watch—one hour per week or four hours per night? What kind of food do you like—are you a health nut or junk food junkie? How will you use the Lord's Day? (It will be one-seventh of your life together.) Do you have things you enjoy doing together?

What level of financial and material expectations do you have? How is money handled? What percentage of your money are you now giving to the Lord? What kind of neighborhood do you anticipate living in—inner-city row home or suburban mansion? What geographical location—Uganda or Vermont or New York City?

What level and kinds of church involvement do you desire? Will you go to church once a week, or will you spend four nights a week in church activities? How much time do you spend devotionally?

Are you basically agreed in your theology? How do you view the authority of Scripture, Calvinism, the charismatic movement, baptism, eschatology, etc.?

What are your views and attitudes towards the roles of men and women, husband and wife? Will both husband and wife work? How should decisions be made?

How many children do you want? None? Two? The more the merrier? How should children be loved and cared for? How should they be disciplined? What are the "disciplinable offenses"? Who does what with the children?

How often will you visit parents? Where do you like to spend vacations and holidays? How much will you do with other friends besides each other?

This is a sampling of the kinds of questions we believe couples contemplating marriage should ask themselves. Perhaps you can think of others!

We'll say it again: Are you heading in the same direction in your lives? Sometimes this is a hard question for a young couple to take seriously. It is easy to say, "Yeah, yeah, we're going in the same direction; we'll work it out." But the present direction is the best predictor of the future.

Stand back and take a good, realistic look at yourselves. Are there any "red flags" that indicate that some of these important issues have not been resolved in you or the other person? Resist the temptation to whitewash these questions! On the other hand, are there "green flags" indicating that your lives *are* moving more and more in the same direction? If your answer is "yes," be encouraged! Vows of marriage can be made with great joy when you are confident that you both are "leaving" and are ready to "cleave" together for the rest of your lives.

For Discussion
Talk through the above questions!

4. What Do Those Who Know You Well Think of Your Relationship?

We often do not see ourselves as well as others see us. And sometimes we are so starstruck with another person that we do not see the whole picture very clearly.

While we don't let others make our decisions for us, the Bible is clear that we are not to rely only on ourselves for wisdom. Proverbs 15:22 says, "Plans fail for lack of counsel, but with many advisers they succeed." Romans 15:14 (CCNT) tells us that as we grow in the knowledge of God, we become "competent to counsel" each other.

It can be tough to balance the fact that you *need* the counsel of others while at the same time you must make the final decision. We usually see three kinds of people in this regard.

First, there is the overly independent "Lone Ranger," who refuses any input and counsel from others. He says, "I make my own decisions."

Second, we often see the overly dependent "slave-to-others'-opinions," who looks for others to make the decision for him. Such a person is blown back and forth by the various opinions of others and afraid to make decisions.

The third kind of person, the "biblically free person," is able to use counsel well. These people are confident that the final decision is their own, but they are also aware that they are limited and fallible. They know their need for Christ and for others. Thus they are free to invite any and all counsel that might help make a wise decision.

Whom Should You Ask for Counsel?

First, ask people who know you. People who have seen you and your potential mate in action together can make helpful observations.

Second, ask people who know what makes a marriage work. Choose people who are experienced, "older and wiser" than you are, whose opinions and wisdom you respect. Even non-Christians—parents, relatives, family friends, a college roommate, a work mate or employer—may have perspectives worth considering.

Third, ask people who will help you look at marriage from a Christian point of view. Your pastor, an elder from your church, a fellowship group leader, and wise Christian friends can help you think biblically about what is involved in marriage. Getting specifically biblical pre-engagement counseling is extremely important, whether done informally or formally.

Fourth, ask your parents. They know you. They have lived longer than you. They care about what happens to you.

We must say another word about talking with your parents. Many young adults have a strained relationship with their parents. Perhaps in childhood or adolescence you developed a pattern of ignoring or despising your parents' counsel and ideas. Or perhaps one or both parents sinned against you by criticism, physical abuse, divorce, or other ungodly behavior. There is now a distance between you and your parents. At this stage in life, as you anticipate getting married, you have a wonderful opportunity to seek to heal the breach. It is a time to attempt to talk to your parents in depth, to listen to their ideas, to show respect, to take them seriously.

Tying up the loose ends of your past helps ensure that you will not bring "emotional baggage" into the new marriage. Reconciliation with your parents will ease your spouse's entry into your family. Your spouse won't have to suffer the tensions and strains of your past.

There may be cases where such reconciliation is impossible, but that in itself is a situation meriting earnest prayer and frank discussion. In most cases we have seen the opposite. Both parents and child experience a new adult-to-adult closeness and respect. Walls of mistrust and hurt on both sides are melted by new love and understanding. The marriage then becomes an occasion for "giving away the bride" with great joy. Go with humility to your parents. God has many kinds of good gifts for his children, and healing the "generation gap" is one of them.

How should you weigh the counsel you receive? A lot of the best counsel you will receive does not come in the form of direct advice; rather, it helps you clarify the issues. It helps you understand your motives, reservations, and goals. Seeking counsel is not the same as taking a Gallup Poll—"seven out of twelve people say I should marry Sue, so I'll go for it." Rather, you seek feedback from others to inform what will be *your* decision, a decision you want to make wisely.

Sometimes someone may raise questions or objections improperly, or may pressure you to go ahead. You may not be able to satisfy everybody. The questions people raise may be unjust; criticisms may be unfair; opinions may be bigoted; you may be pressured to go forward or hold back for bad reasons. But you should be able to answer, to your own satisfaction, the issues raised even by people with whom you disagree.

There is a lot of bad counsel around. It can

say "go" for bad reasons: "She's cute." "He's going to be rich." "The Lord has told me you should marry him/her." It can say "no go" for bad reasons: "You'll lose your bachelor life and be tied down." "She's not Lithuanian like you are." "I have a check in my spirit about it." You want to weigh the reasons people give for the course they think is best.

There is also good counsel to be had. Good counsel helps you carefully and prayerfully think through the decision. It sorts out whether your main reasons for marrying are self-centered or if you know how to commit yourself to love someone else. Good counsel helps you identify potential problem areas and work on them before you are so committed that it would be an embarrassment to pull back.

Good counsel helps you know you can solve problems biblically and face difficulties. It helps you know you are moving in the same direction. Good counsel helps you see your strengths and Christ's strength and so gives you confidence to enter marriage with joy and optimism.

"The way of a fool seems right to him, but a wise man listens to advice" (Prov. 12:15). What do others who know you well think of your relationship? What do they think of your maturity? Of your plans and goals? Don't be too proud or too timid to ask for help.

For Discussion
1. Whose counsel would be helpful to us? Make a list!
2. How can we schedule times with these people?

5. Do You Want to Marry This Person? Are You Willing to Accept Each Other Just as You Are?

The Bible tells us that the decision to marry is a choice we make. The final questions you should ask yourself are, "Do I want to marry this person?" and "Does this person want to marry me?"

Sometimes people think this kind of question is unspiritual, as though God must miraculously and mystically reveal whether and whom you should marry. Marriage *is* a miracle! And God does lead his people! But he leads by giving us wisdom and allowing us to make real choices. Getting married is your choice. You are the one who will affirm vows and say "I do." No one—and no "leading"—can constrain or compel you to make these vows.

Likewise, you must respect the other person's right and responsibility to make his or her own decision about you. We are not robots or puppets of each other or even of the Holy Spirit. We are children who live by faith, who have a tender and personal Shepherd and Father. We make choices based on biblical wisdom. The questions we have been asking presuppose that *you* will be the one to make the final commitment.

We stress this personal choice factor because we have seen people become very confused and led into unwarranted marriages because they were told by someone else, "I know it is God's will for you to marry so-and-so," or because their parents or someone else pressured them. We have also seen people paralyzed with indecision because they thought they needed some special sign to confirm whether or not they should marry. The first four questions we asked are meant to guarantee that you do not rush into marriage just because you want to. But there does come a time when it is essential to ask yourself, "Do I *want* to?"

First Corinthians 7:25–40 is the lengthiest Scripture passage that explicitly discusses how people decide to get married. It is filled with phrases such as: "He should do as he wants. He is not sinning" (v. 36); "The man who has settled the matter in his own mind, who is under no compulsion but has control over his own will, and who has made up his mind . . ." (v. 37); "She is free to marry anyone she wishes, but he must belong to the Lord" (v. 39).

Could it be any clearer? God expects you to make the decision. And God promises to bless you and work out his will in your life *through* your decisions.

We have known couples who worked through the first four questions, and the whole process seemed to be "full speed ahead." But when we got to this question, after private, thoughtful reflection, one of the persons has said, "I really don't want to marry at this time." The only reason things got this far was "My mother really wants me to get married" or "My boyfriend has pressured me that it's right" or "We had sex and I feel guilty and obligated, as though we were married already" or "Everyone says we look great together and we're made for each other, but . . ." or "I've been afraid that if I pass up this chance I might never get another one."

Fear, guilt, social pressure, or a twisted sense of fate are not reasons to get married. It is important to bring to the surface any reservations you may feel. Sometimes the reservations can be dealt with so that you become able to say "yes" with a whole heart. Sometimes the reservations simply stand as a reason to say "no." It is much better to say "no" before engagement than to say twenty years after marriage, "I went to the altar with secret doubts, and I have lived with regrets ever since."

Instead of harboring secret reservations, you want to say a hearty "yes." Jesus says, "Let your 'Yes' be 'Yes,' and your 'No,' 'No' " (Matt. 5:37).

The time to decide whether or not you want to marry is *before* your engagement. We have written these five questions to be part of the *pre-engagement* thinking and counseling of a man and woman who have become friends and want to raise the marriage issue. Too often in our culture, however, engagement is seen as a trial period where "I'm still deciding."

To be sure, engagement doesn't mean that you are married or that the decision is irreversible. Nonetheless, to view engagement as a trial period is quite foolish. Many couples could have avoided the pain and embarrassment of broken engagements if they had honestly asked themselves these questions first. You want your time of engagement to be a time of growing joy and eager anticipation as you make decisions and plans together.

Reservations are not the only things that must be brought to the surface. Remember, your "yes" is to a person, not to a "fantasy woman" or to "the man I hope he will become"! Ask yourself, "Am I willing to accept this person as he or she is? Do I want to marry *this* person?" Make sure that you are not coming to marriage with a hidden agenda, expecting to change the other person once you are married. Are you saying "yes" to a real person, with weaknesses as well as strengths, sins as well as gifts?

It is liberating to say "yes" and mean it. Therefore, we urge you to take time to search your heart and pray to the Lord. "Rejoice in the Lord always. I will say it again: Rejoice! . . . in everything, by prayer and petition, with thanksgiving, present your requests to God" (Phil. 4:4, 6). Use this time to delight in the Lord. Cleanse your motives, and put him first in your life. Be quiet before him, seeking his wisdom. Pour out your heart. Ask his blessing.

Perhaps you should set aside a day for fasting and special prayer beyond your normal prayer times. Think. Ask yourself questions. Ponder the implications of your decision.

On this foundation make your decision,

trusting in the Lord's goodness to his children. " 'For I know the plans I have for you,' declares the LORD, 'plans to prosper you and not to harm you, plans to give you hope and a future' " (Jer. 29:11).

For Personal Reflection
1. Do you want to marry this person?
2. Are you willing to accept this person exactly as he or she is?

Conclusion

Marriage is one of the greatest gifts of God to mankind. The union of the bride and bridegroom is rightly one of the supreme symbols of joy. We pray that God will lead many of you to experience this joy.

The time that you spend in reflecting on and discussing the questions we have raised is time that will be well spent. This is more than going through a "check list." It will be a time of discovery about the other person that will allow you to grow in your love for him or her. You are investing time in your future joy. The Bible says, "Godliness has value for all things . . . for both the present life and the life to come" (1 Tim. 4:8). Each of these questions will help you to grow in "godliness," in thinking accurately and living skillfully. You will think about marriage with the living God—who gave his beloved Son, Jesus, to become your husband—at the center of your thoughts.

Someday death will separate you and your spouse. But you will be prepared even for that. You will have your joy firmly set in the life to come. If Christ is at the center of your life and marriage now, then even marriage itself will not be your goal in life. In hardships, even in death, you will have resources of hope, strength, and encouragement.

Do you grasp that there is someone you are to love even more than your own husband or wife? Jesus said, "If anyone comes to me and does not hate his father and mother, his wife and children, his brothers and sisters—yes, even his own life—he cannot be my disciple" (Luke 14:26).

Perhaps you think this is a curious way to end a discussion of whether or not you should get married! But hear Jesus out. Jesus loves his bride with an intensity and depth that is unequaled (see Eph. 5:2, 25 as well as Rev. 19:6–9!). A disciple of Jesus is someone learning how to love in the same way. If you love Jesus Christ more than your wife or husband, you will learn how to love your spouse with something of his intensity and depth. This is one of those beautiful paradoxes of biblical truth. If you love and want your spouse more than anything, you will end up selfish, fearful, bitter or disillusioned. If you love Jesus more than anything else, you will really love and enjoy your spouse. You will be someone worth marrying! And that, after all, is the biggest question of all. Will you be a source of gladness to another? With Jesus' help—YES!

David Powlison *is the editor of the* Journal of Biblical Counseling *and a member of the faculty and counseling staff at the Christian Counseling and Educational Foundation in Glenside, Pennsylvania.*

John Yenchko *is pastor of North Shore Community Church in Oyster Bay, New York.*

RCL Ministry Booklets

A.D.D.: Wandering Minds and Wired Bodies, by Edward T. Welch

Anger: Escaping the Maze, by David Powlison

Angry at God? Bring Him Your Doubts and Questions, by Robert D. Jones

Bad Memories: Getting Past Your Past, by Robert D. Jones

Depression: The Way Up When You Are Down, by Edward T. Welch

Domestic Abuse: How to Help, by David Powlison, Paul David Tripp, and Edward T. Welch

Forgiveness: "I Just Can't Forgive Myself!" by Robert D. Jones

God's Love: Better than Unconditional, by David Powlison

Guidance: Have I Missed God's Best? by James C. Petty

Homosexuality: Speaking the Truth in Love, by Edward T. Welch

"Just One More": When Desires Don't Take No for an Answer, by Edward T. Welch

Marriage: Whose Dream? by Paul David Tripp

Motives: "Why Do I Do the Things I Do?" by Edward T. Welch

OCD: Freedom for the Obsessive-Compulsive, by Michael R. Emlet

COUNSELING RESOURCES

Price: $14.99

"David Powlison has profoundly impacted my ministry by teaching me the discipline of seeing life through the lens of Scripture rather than the other way around. The crumbs from Dave's table—his most casual comments—have nourished me for years. This is a feast of biblical insight."   —KEN SANDE

"Powlison urges counselors to speak directly to people rather than use abstractions. In this excellent book he takes a number of Bible passages and speaks them right into our hearts. Reading this is a rich experience for counselors and for everyone who wants to apply God's Word to his or her life."   —JOHN FRAME

Counseling Resources

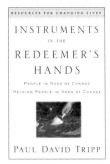

Price: $16.99

"A wonderful reminder that everyone who belongs to Jesus can help others. God gave us to each other! This is a wise and helpful book that should change your life and that of the church. Read it! You'll be glad."

—Steve Brown

"Tripp is a careful and skillful physician of the heart. He unites a loving heart with a mind trained to the Scriptures. This book is a great companion for pastors and counselors. It will guide anyone who wants to give real help to others, the saving help that is found in Christ's redeeming work."

—Richard D. Phillips

COUNSELING RESOURCES

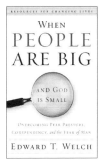

Price: $14.99

"Ed Welch is a good physician of the soul. This book is enlightening, convicting, and encouraging. I highly recommend it."

—JERRY BRIDGES

". . . refreshingly biblical. . . . brimming with helpful, readable, practical insight."

—JOHN MACARTHUR

"Readable and refreshing. . . . goes to the heart of an issue immobilizing the church. Exposes and repudiates the trivia of therapeutic theology with wisdom and compassion."

—SUSAN HUNT